Building BULK

**Edward Connors, Peter Grymkowski,
Tim Kimber, and Michael J. B. McCormick**

CONTEMPORARY BOOKS

Library of Congress Cataloging-in-Publication Data

Building bulk / Edward Connors . . . [et al.] : with photographs by
    Irvin J. Gelb.
       p.   cm. — (Gold's gym essentials series : bk. 1)
    Includes index.
    ISBN 0-8092-2789-4
    1. Bodybuilding.   2. Muscle strength.   I. Connors, Ed.
II. Series.
GV546.5.B858   1999
646.7′5—dc21   98-43699
                                                  CIP

In no way does the appearance of any of the models in this book represent that
they endorse Gold's Gym or the methods of training or diet included herein.

Cover design by Todd Petersen
Cover and interior photographs copyright © Irvin J. Gelb
Interior design by Hespenheide Design

Published by Contemporary Books
A division of NTC/Contemporary Publishing Group, Inc.
4255 West Touhy Avenue, Lincolnwood (Chicago), Illinois 60646-1975 U.S.A.
Printed in the United States of America
International Standard Book Number: 0-8092-2789-4
99 00 01 02 03 04 VL 18 17 16 15 14 13 12 11 10 9 8 7 6 5 4 3 2 1

CONTENTS

Building BULK

INTRODUCTION

For over fifty years, bodybuilders have pursued the single-minded goal of increasing their muscle mass. By definition, the sport of bodybuilding involves the effort to increase the size of your body. This first in the new series of Gold's Gym bodybuilding books contains successful principles to help you reach your full physical potential.

The title of this book is *Building Bulk*; however, it could just as easily have been titled *Getting Big*, *Total Muscular Growth*, or *Monstrous Muscles*. The title doesn't matter, because every bodybuilder understands the topic—more muscle. Bodybuilders share the common interest of seeking to maximize their muscular size. This deep desire to add pounds of lean muscle connects all bodybuilders; there is no such thing as the bodybuilder who doesn't want to get bigger. Granted, some bodybuilders may need to stay within a certain weight class, but they nonetheless attempt to pack on as much muscle as possible.

Whatever your initial physical condition is, there are incredible gains waiting for you if you apply sound training and recuperation habits. Over time, the human body is capable of radical changes in physical appearance.

The following factors are major determinants in how much muscular size you can pack on and how long it will take:

Jay Cutler

- age
- gender
- age when started weight lifting (i.e., sixteen vs. twenty-nine)
- length of time weight lifting
- genetics
- daily protein intake

Although these are important determinants of your physical potential, the intensity of your bodybuilding dream and your commitment to that dream are the most important factors for success.

No one can definitively predict how much muscle you'll be able to gain. The outcome is in your hands and no one else's. Few bodybuilders entering the sport each year are going to win a pro card and compete as such; this a reality of life. However, gaining 10, 25, or even 50 pounds is possible if you fully commit to the information presented in the following chapters.

In the effort to explain bodybuilding, there is a tendency to explore every possible aspect of the subject. However, in practical reality there is a limited amount of information that will help you reach your bodybuilding goals. Thus, while we could have expanded the workouts in the last chapter to include every possible variation and arrangement, producing

Ronnie Coleman

Lee Priest

more than 200 different exercise structures, the thirty-one workouts we include here more than serve the purpose of framing the arena for growth. Trying to understand the vast amount of information available about bodybuilding can easily result in information overload, with the forest obscuring the trees. The purpose of this book is to present the essential information for muscular growth, ensuring that you have the tools you will need to succeed.

Every pound of new muscle you gain will require an increase in your daily nutritional intake. Both the macronutrient and micronutrient components of your eating and supplementing programs will be needed in greater abundance. These increased requirements are best handled on a scheduled basis that is linked to specific amounts of increased body weight. For example, you might increase your protein and total calories by 10 percent with each 5 pounds gained. For purposes of discussion, let's assume your initial intake of daily calories is 3,000 and protein is 200 grams. At a starting body weight of 200 pounds, you would increase your calories the

Jay Cutler

Debbie Kruck

day that the scale reflects a new weight of 205 pounds. At this point, you would increase your daily intake to 3,300 calories and 220 grams of protein.

Before you embark upon a serious bodybuilding regimen, ask yourself the following questions:

- How much food do I eat to maintain my current body weight?
- How much weight do I want to gain?
- About how long will it take to gain this amount?
- How much additional food will I need to sustain this growth?
- When will I need to increase my calorie intake and by how much?
- What is my current training volume?
- What areas of my physique need the most attention?
- How can I change my training to stimulate growth?

Your task is to personally investigate the answers to these questions. Rev your mental engine and warm up your mind. There's lots of work to be done, so let's get busy and grow!

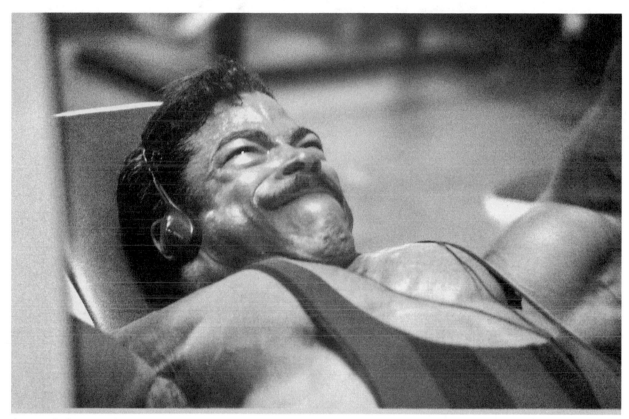

Aaron Baker

Ronnie Coleman

BODYBUILDING BASICS

MOTIVATION

In bodybuilding, once you accurately assess your genetic potential you are limited only by your desire. The playgrounds of the world are filled with hundreds of unrealized Mr. and Ms. Olympias. The champions are the ones who match their particular genetic strengths with even greater amounts of desire and motivation!

Motivation is your best weapon in the war against smallness. When a bodybuilder first starts to train, growth can be predicted. Most bodybuilders go through an initial burst of growth regardless of the effectiveness of their diets and training. To an extent, the initial gains that bodybuilders experience are automatic, as though the muscles self-inflate from merely going to the gym. Later in your career as a bodybuilder, you will need far more thought and introspection to continue improving.

The day will arrive sooner than later when you'll be tired of eating constantly (or some other vital component to growth), and you'll be tempted to back off from training. It's your degree of desire and motivation that will either pull you through the challenge or allow you to shortchange yourself.

A successful initial period of growth is vital for long-term success as a bodybuilder. This is the time when your emotional self

Milos Sarcev

becomes conditioned to expect positive results from your bodybuilding efforts. It is often during this time that the full magnitude of your self-empowerment dawns on you. It becomes apparent that you literally can transform your physical appearance via bodybuilding.

GOALS

Most bodybuilders can quickly identify the personal goal that provides their motivation and drive for commitment and success. Few of us are completely satisfied with our physical appearance. Whether you need to reduce your body fat or increase your body weight, the first required step for results is action.

Bodybuilding provides the tools to accomplish what the best of medicine cannot: a complete physical transformation from dissatisfaction toward fulfillment of your potential. The fat become lean, and the skinny fill out their frames. Miracles occur every day in the more than 500 Gold's Gyms worldwide!

Creating Effective Goals

Your bodybuilding goals will, in large part, determine your ultimate success. To maximize the effectiveness of your goals, you should:

- write them down, preferably in a notebook
- update them on a regular basis
- share them with people whose opinion you trust and value

Bodybuilding is a sport based upon setting goals. Significant growth is the outcome of countless small goals continually set, accomplished, and revised in an upward cycle of progress. When establishing goals, record them regularly in writing, using definite and specific statements. "I'm gonna get huge as a house" is a vague and ineffective goal. Effective goals are clear and concrete and state exactly what you're aiming for. An effective goal statement is, "I will gain 10 pounds without any change in my degree of muscular definition." Over time, you

Porter Cottrell

Ronnie Coleman

might expand the goal with more specific details: "I will gain 10 pounds in the next six months without any change in my degree of muscular definition by training consistently and eating 1.5 grams of protein per pound of body weight every day."

Articulating your goals clearly and specifically, writing them down, and periodically revising them will be crucial to your success. In the long run, it will be the day-to-day adherence to your goals that will make or break your efforts as a bodybuilder.

SELF-ASSESSMENT

The process of a physical self-inventory is strongly recommended in order to align your motives, goals, and strategies for optimum results. This self-scrutiny should be undertaken with thorough

Claude Groux

and rigorous honesty. Having an accurate understanding of your body's positive and negative characteristics protects against training under self-deceptive conditions. Believing that you are ready to compete in a contest after your first four months of training or trying to gain 15 pounds when your body fat is already at 29 percent are both examples of self-deceptive behavior.

B. J. Quinn

Body Weight

The first issue at hand is how much you weigh. Generally, bodybuilders quantify most of their goals in terms of body weight. It is important to always weigh yourself on the same scale and at the same time of day, since scales vary and one's body weight fluctuates throughout the day. To track your weight accurately, we suggest checking it every seven days.

Body Composition

Technology provides several options for the next step in self-assessment: determining your proportion of muscle (lean tissue) to fat (adipose tissue), known as body fat testing or body composition assessment.

Skin fold assessments obtained with dermal calipers are the least expensive and least accurate option. Recent advances in technology have produced electrical resistance measurement, which is moderately accurate. Electrical resistance testing is usually less than fifty dollars and is available for home and commercial use. Other reliable methods are total body immersion and the K-40 isotope method.

The high-end body composition measuring tool is a DEXA, or dual-energy x-ray absorptiometry, unit. DEXA units produce low-energy x-rays that, when used with exclusive software, indicate variations in body density. This form of measurement yields an extremely accurate set of comparisons among one's amounts of muscle, fat, and bone. Currently, DEXA units cost well over $100,000 and, therefore, are found only in hospitals and clinics. DEXA unit assessments cost a hundred dollars or more and require an appointment. However, the accuracy of this form of assessment makes the price worth it for many bodybuilders. DEXA unit technology was originally developed to measure bone density to test for osteoporosis.

Kevin Christie

Body composition testing should not be used as a bragging tool: "I'm 250 pounds and have only 3.5 percent body fat." In reality, body-fat percentages below 5 percent are unheard of. *Extremely* lean bodybuilders dip into the single digits at contest time. During the balance of the year, however, the vast majority of male professional bodybuilders stay around 12 to 15 percent body fat. In the case of female bodybuilders, the percentage of body fat is slightly to moderately higher than for males of similar size and age.

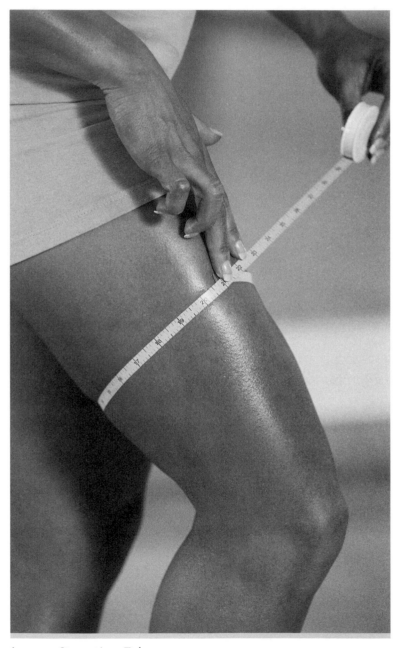

Lovena Stamatiou-Tuley

Photographs

Bodybuilding contests are judged on appearance. This fact explains why it is a good idea to keep a photographic record of your physique. Looking at the results from a twenty-four-exposure roll of film is an exercise in brutal honesty. If the pictures reveal a lean, hard, and dense musculature, congratulations! If they make you uncomfortable, then they should motivate you to become leaner. Photos are one of the best tools to use for self-assessment. The following are some suggestions for obtaining accurate photos:

- Use the same camera.
- Have the same person take the pictures.
- Take the pictures at the same time of day.
- Take the pictures at the same location.

If possible, obtain pictures of yourself at fourteen-day intervals. If this is not doable, try to take them at least once a month. Photos are unlikely to deceive if they are repeated under the same conditions and compared over time. Pictures enable you to decide if quality progress is evident or not. Unlike the comments of well-meaning friends and family, pictures are objective and lead less to falsehoods.

Video

It's a great idea to capture yourself on video in addition to photos. The variations between the two forms of image add to the information you have to gauge your progress.

KEEPING RECORDS

One of the best habits a bodybuilder can develop is keeping a daily record or journal. The value of accurate

Armin Scholz

Armin Scholz

self-awareness in an individual sport like bodybuilding cannot be overstated. There are no stopwatches or end zones in bodybuilding. You have your physical appearance as your accomplishment. Whether you call it a written record, log, journal, notebook, or diary is your choice. What is important is that you record information about your training to use for self-evaluation and improvement.

The following categories list areas that affect, for better or worse, the ultimate success of today's bodybuilders. The last item should not be overlooked. Ignoring the reality of one's living situation and resources is a serious mistake not uncommon in the world of bodybuilding. Tom Platz wrote of this aspect of bodybuilding life in the early 1980s in one of his superlative training guides. He stressed the importance of personal commitment, adequate financial resources, and social or family support in the life of a bodybuilder trying to initiate a competitive career.

Training
- days of the week
- time of day
- where you train
- who you train with
- how to split the body parts
- exercises in each workout
- length of each workout
- number of sets and reps in each workout

Nutrition
- times of meals
- content of meals
- nutrient content
- supplements

Recovery
- sleep
- stress
- active recovery techniques: stretching, massage, icing

Reality
- financial resources
- work
- family commitments
- family support

Aaron Maddron

Melvin Anthony

The following chart is meant to copied, reproduced, and inserted into whatever recording system you intend to utilize. Arbitrarily jotting down thoughts, facts, and figures is not likely to be useful in the long run. It pays to understand the value of specific information. Be specific and stay specific!

The results you enjoy as a bodybuilder are locked step for step with your personal commitment to excellence. Your efforts must be 100 percent and acted upon day after day, year after year. Growth becomes near predictable when the following conditions are met on a consistent basis:

- Eat the required amount of food (this is not as easy as it sounds).
- Drink proper quantities of water.
- Take appropriate supplements.
- Get adequate sleep.
- Train consistently.
- Engage in active recovery techniques such as massage therapy, cold/heat therapy, and stretching.

TO BE COPIED AND USED IN NOTEBOOK!

DAILY SELF-ASSESSMENT

Date:
_____

Body weight:
_____

Hours of sleep last night:
_____

Description of today's workout (include exercises, sets, reps, and other comments):
_____
_____
_____
_____

Meals, snacks, and supplements (include details about types of food, amounts, times, etc.):
_____
_____
_____
_____

What my mood was:
_____
_____
_____
_____

How I felt physically:
_____
_____
_____
_____

Porter Cottrell

Claude Groux

PUTTING IT TOGETHER FOR THE NEXT STEP

Your success as a bodybuilder will ultimately depend on the strength of your motivation, goals, and self-assessment. It is crucial that you attend to each aspect of your growth and understand how they are interrelated. For example, your goal may be to compete in bodybuilding, but your self-assessment indicates that you're carrying too much excess fat and need to tighten up on your body composition percentages. The correct approach in this case is to take sufficient time at the start of your bodybuilding career to work diligently on your definition. The process of shedding excess body fat will make your muscles appear to be larger because of the increased delineation among body parts. At the risk of oversimplifying the facts, your abdominal muscles are generally the most reliable reference for assessing your body fat condition. If photos of yourself show abdominal muscles, you are ready to grow immediately, but if no abdominal muscles are visible you'll need to tighten your musculature first by reducing your body fat level.

Dave Hughes

Gunther Schlierkamp

MUSCLE GROWTH

The information in this chapter is essential to achieving your maximum growth patterns. The better informed a bodybuilder is about what his or her body is being pushed to accomplish, the more predictable a successful result becomes.

Perhaps the most remarkable aspect of bodybuilding is the rapid and often dramatic physical transformation that can occur. In general, the human machine responds to bodybuilding, or progressive resistance training, in a predictable pattern that involves two distinct phases: first-stage growth and muscle maturation.

FIRST-STAGE GROWTH

First-stage growth is sometimes referred to as the "initial burst." During this time, the majority of bodybuilders gain significant weight, and the demarcations of muscle appear. Often, this first burst of weight gain yields newly acquired muscle and, more significantly, extra body fat. This type of mixed lean/fat growth is nothing to become discouraged over. It is, however, indicative of your body's individual metabolism and merits attention as you plan your diet and routine. This period of initial success may last up to a year.

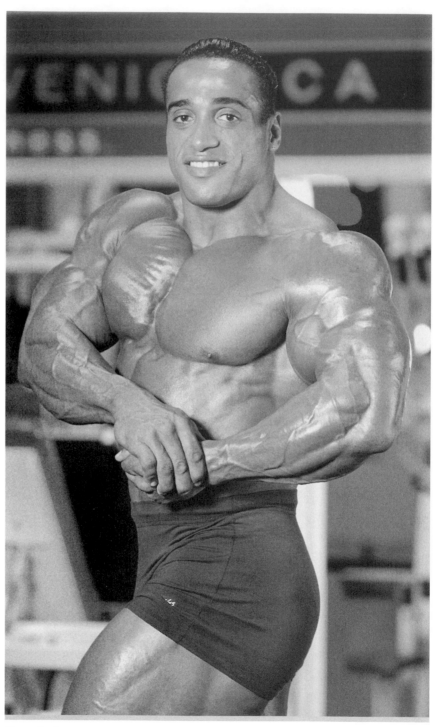

Dennis James

Less obvious than increasing body weight are the psychological shifts that occur. The rapid pace of weight gain during the early stages of training provides powerful motivation for the bodybuilder. Gaining those first pounds is electrifying! There is no doubt or debate that the scale now reads 200 pounds and no longer only 195. You become more focused and dedicated from this accomplishment because it proves that success is within your reach. The confidence that this first-stage growth brings will help you rise to the next level of growth, which will require 100 percent commitment from you.

MUSCLE MATURATION

Muscle maturation is evidenced by a density of musculature with minimal body fat. The quality of size you add during this period serves as the foundation for successful competition as a bodybuilder. This stage of maturation typically happens in the second year of committed training.

Jonathan Lawson

Armin Scholz

Successful bodybuilders make every attempt to always sustain a dense and tight physique. A lean, tight appearance is evidence of muscular maturity.

REASONABLE EXPECTATIONS FOR GROWTH

Gains in body weight never come in a steady stream but seemingly in bursts. The pattern of growth is one of significant size and weight gain, followed by a refractory period with little change in weight. As you begin serious bodybuilding, it is important to have realistic expectations for growth. Here are general guidelines as to how much weight you might expect to pack on:

- Five to 10 pounds per year is normal.
- Ten pounds or more is reason to be happy.
- More than 15 pounds per year is phenomenal.

As an example, we'll use a fictional 175-pound male novice bodybuilder who is twenty-five years of age. During the first year of training, he packs on an additional 5 percent of lean body weight. At the end of the year, he weighs in at 184 pounds. This is a gain of 9 pounds, which is a reasonable goal to expect to meet during the first twelve months of training. His rate of muscle gaining in the next three years continues in the range of 1 to 3 percent yearly. Of course, growth is dependent on the degree of commitment and dedication you put into the process. If you train with enough intensity, you can achieve growth percentages better than those of our fictional bodybuilder. For

Armin Scholz

Bill Davey

example, if you start out at 175 pounds, it is possible to achieve 200 pounds in two years. A weight of 200 pounds certainly is a huge jump from 175 pounds; however, it seems more feasible when you consider that this additional body weight works out to be just a little over 1 pound per month for twenty-four months. When viewed from this perspective, massive muscle size becomes available to everyone. Here is a summary of realistic rates of weight gain:

Year 1:   3–7 percent
Years 2–4:   1–3 percent

ENVIRONMENT FOR GROWTH

After training, the body has incurred a small amount of muscle structure damage that must be repaired. It is this repair process that produces growth. Significant growth occurs over an extended period of time. The repair process produces growth under conditions of adequate nutrition, rest from activity, sleep, and hormonal influence. If you cut corners on any of these conditions, you will not maximize your physical potential. Over five years, the bodybuilder who is consistent with training, diet, and rest will gain 2 pounds for every 1 pound that a corner-cutting bodybuilder gains.

Sleep

The impact of sleep on bodybuilding is tremendous. The importance of getting enough sleep every day cannot be overstated, since it is essential to provide your body's metabolism with adequate rest. The number of sleep hours required varies greatly from person to person. Generally, eight hours is sufficient for most bodybuilders; however, this is an area that only you can accurately gauge. A good rule to follow is the harder you train a muscle the more rest it requires to repair itself.

Sleep is the time when your body's repair process goes into high gear. Shortchanging your sleep is taking a step in the wrong

Remi Zuri

direction. If circumstances prevent you from getting a full night's sleep, then make every reasonable effort to take naps during the day. Many of the world's biggest bodybuilders are grabbing naps whenever the opportunity allows.

PSYCHOLOGY OF CONSISTENT GROWTH

In bodybuilding, your mind is the all-important link to success. If you are uncertain of your goals, you are drastically reducing your prospects for a successful bodybuilding career. The power of self-belief cannot be overstated. If you want to achieve a certain size or condition, then take time to actually visualize yourself as you intend to be. The mind enlists the body as its tool to build with. Your body will not grow on its own. It must be consistently prodded along by the intensity of your mind's determination and image of yourself at a heavier body weight.

Jay Cutler

3 EATING FOR LEAN GROWTH

Training involves relatively few of the 168 hours in a week. Outside of the gym, you're left with approximately 96 percent of the week for recuperation. Your success as a bodybuilder will be partially determined by how well you apply sound nutritional knowledge. Efficient nutrition awareness involves understanding how to best consume, assimilate, and use nutrients.

Optimum muscular growth occurs under conditions of balanced consumption of both macronutrients and micronutrients. Macronutrients are proteins, carbohydrates, fats, and water. Micronutrients are vitamins, minerals, trace elements, and other minor but still vital metabolic substrates.

CARBOHYDRATES

The word *carbohydrate* combines the Latin *carbo*, meaning *coal*, and the Greek *hydro*, meaning *water*. Carbohydrates are any of a group of organic compounds, the most important being the saccharides, starch, cellulose, and gum. Carbohydrates constitute the main source of energy for all body functions, particularly brain functions, and are necessary for the metabolism of other nutrients.

Brad Baker

Carbohydrates are synthesized by all green plants and in the body are either absorbed immediately or stored in the form of glycogen. Grains, vegetables, fruits, and legumes are the major sources of carbohydrates. They can also be manufactured in the body from some amino acids and the glycerol component of fats.

Carbohydrates are the body's main fuel source. Fats and proteins also contribute to the energy pool but at lesser amounts. For bodybuilding, carbohydrates supply the most accessible energy. Though the largest contributor in terms of hourly provision of energy substrates, carbohydrates store only 2 percent of the body's total fuel reserves, while stored fat contains 80 percent and protein (skeletal muscle) accounts for the remaining 18 percent. Since each gram of carbohydrate is stored in the body with 4 grams of water and stored fat requires no water, the body stores fat more easily and thus relies on fat as its main source of reserve energy.

Brad Baker

Carbohydrate Structure

Carbohydrates are classified as mono-, di-, or polysaccharides. Indigestible, or fibrous, carbohydrates are classified as dietary fiber. The dietary carbohydrates fall into two categories: simple sugars and complex carbohydrates.

Thea Majorova

Simple Sugars

There are two categories of sugars: monosaccharides and disaccharides. A monosaccharide is a single sugar, such as glucose, fructose, or galactose. A disaccharide is a double sugar, such as sucrose (table sugar) or lactose.

Complex Carbohydrates

Polysaccharides are carbohydrates containing three or more molecules of simple carbohydrates. Some examples of polysaccharides are dextrins, starches, glycogens, and celluloses. Sources for polysaccharides are grain products, legumes, potatoes, and other vegetables.

Carbohydrate Metabolism

The metabolism of carbohydrates involves the following three processes: (1) glycogenesis—the synthesis of glycogen from glucose, (2) glyconeogenesis—the formation of

Jay Cutler

glycogen from fatty acids and proteins, and (3) glycolysis—the breaking down of glucose and other sugars for use as energy.

Your carbohydrate metabolism depends largely on the level of blood glucose, or circulating carbohydrates, in your body. This, in turn, is dictated by the timing and nutrient composition of your last meal. Blood glucose, or sugar, is generally at its lowest level in the early morning hours because you have undergone essentially a seven- to nine-hour fast without any new supply of ingested fuel for the needed maintenance of your blood glucose level. The body's source of fuel in this postabsorptive state (fast) is drawn 75 percent from glycolysis and 25 percent from gluconeogenesis.

Upon awakening, your body is at its most efficient for utilizing fat as energy: hence the expression "ride early and empty." These are the hours of highest natural growth-hormone production. During contest preparation or other periods of peak conditioning, it is a good idea to perform your daily aerobics immediately upon waking up and without any food.

Carbohydrates and Insulin

Insulin is a hormone secreted by the pancreas. The release of insulin is directed by increased levels of glucose and amino acids in the blood. Insulin maintains the metabolism of glucose along with the intermediary metabolism of fats and proteins. Insulin lowers blood glucose levels and promotes transport and entry of glucose and amino acids into the muscle cells and other tissues.

Effective Carbohydrate Intake

Simply counting fat grams and considering carbohydrates to be a "safe" food works for only about 1 to 2 percent of bodybuilders. The rest of us have learned the hard way that nutrition is all about balance. Healthy adults demonstrate increased storage of ingested carbohydrates in the form of muscle glycogen when the carbohydrates are consumed between four to six hours after waking up. As the day progresses, the ability or tendency to store

Jay Cutler

Thea Majorova

carbohydrates decreases. We suggest consuming more carbohydrates early in the day and increasing protein consumption as the day progresses.

We include the glycemic index for foods to help you accurately structure your carbohydrate consumption. It is designed around the principle that higher glycemic index (GI) numbered foods produce the largest release of insulin and the subsequent rapid lowering of the initially increased blood glucose level. This massive burst of insulin and the ensuing blood sugar rise and then drop is known as a "blood sugar spike."

For best control over your blood sugar level, attempt as best as possible to consume foods with a low GI number. There is evidence that consistent control over your blood glucose level through structured consumption of low glycemic foods assists in achieving and maintaining lower levels of body fat. The *exception* to this guideline is the two- to three-hour period after completing your training. During this window of opportunity, your body's ability to store carbohydrates as glycogen is increased, and amino acid uptake into the muscles is elevated. During this 120- to 180-

minute time frame, the goal is to pump both carbohydrates and protein into the muscles, which are in a state of increased sensitivity to the effects of insulin.

Glycemic Index for Common Foods

Food	Index	Food	Index
Peanuts	13	White pasta	50
Soybeans	15	Sweet potatoes	51
Fructose	20	Potato chips	51
Cherries	23	Green peas	51
Plums	25	Bran	51
Grapefruit	26	Sweet corn	59
Peaches	26	Sucrose	59
Sausage	28	Bananas	62
Lentils	29	Beets	64
Kidney beans	29	Raisins	64
Skim milk	32	Shredded wheat	67
Pears	34	White bread	69
Whole milk	34	White rice	70
Plain yogurt	36	White potatoes	70
Lima beans	36	Whole wheat bread	72
Chickpeas	36	Cornflakes	80
Ice cream	36	Instant potatoes	80
Tomatoes	38	Honey	87
Apples	39	Carrots	92
Whole wheat pasta	42	Parsnips	98
Whole grain rye bread	42	Russet potatoes	98
Grapes	45	Glucose	100
Oatmeal	49	Maltose	110

FATS

There are numerous vital roles that fats play in optimal health and growth. Fat provides the body with

Jimmy Lee

- insulation;
- fuel;
- padding for vital organs;
- essential fatty acids; and
- the building blocks for cell membranes.

Fat Metabolism

Fats provide more energy than carbohydrates or protein do. The breaking down, or catabolism, of 1 gram (g) of fat provides 9 kilocalories (kcal) of heat, whereas the catabolism of 1 g of carbohydrate or protein yields 4.1 kcal. Fat catabolism involves a series of chemical reactions, the last stages of which are similar to the final reactions of carbohydrate catabolism.

The body can synthesize only saturated fatty acids. Essential fatty acids are unsaturated molecules that cannot be produced by the body and must be included in the diet. Free fatty acids are fatty acids released by the hydrolysis of triglycerides from body fat stores. Free fatty acids may be used as an immediate source of energy by many organs or converted by the liver into ketone bodies. Fatty acids are also broken down, or catabolized, yielding the required glycerol component for conversion to glucose.

Gunther Schlierkamp

Brad Baker

Hormones, which include insulin, growth hormone, adrenocorticotropic, and glucocorticoids, all control fat metabolism.

Fat Structures

Monosaturated fatty acids have only one double or triple bond per molecule and are found in foods such as almonds, pecans, cashew nuts, peanuts, and olive oil. Polyunsaturated fatty acids have more than one double or triple bond per molecule and are found in foods such as fish, corn, walnuts, sunflower seeds, soybeans, cottonseeds, and safflower oil.

Saturated fatty acids are any of a number of glyceryl esters of certain organic acids in which all the atoms are joined by single bonds. These fats are chiefly of animal origin and are found in beef, lamb, pork, veal, whole-milk products including butter and most cheeses, and a few plant products such as cocoa butter, coconut oil, and palm oil.

Essential fatty acids are polyunsaturated fatty acids such as linoleic acid, alpha-linolenic acid, and arachidonic acid. They are essential in the diet for the proper growth, maintenance, and

Brad Baker

Erik Fromm

functioning of the body. Essential fatty acids are the precursors for the synthesis of prostaglandins and are vital to fat transport, metabolism, and the normal functioning of the endocrine systems.

PROTEIN

Protein is any of a large group of naturally occurring, complex, organic nitrogenous compounds. Each is composed of large combinations of amino acids containing the elements carbon, hydrogen, nitrogen, oxygen, usually sulfur, and occasionally phosphorus, iron, iodine, or other essential constituents of living cells. Within your body, protein is broken down into its amino acid, or peptide structure. Once actively absorbed, a protein's constituents

- help synthesize hormones, neurotransmitters, enzymes, and other biochemicals
- are consumed as energy during periods of intense stress, injury, and caloric deficit

- assist the functioning of the immune system
- help repair existing levels of tissue
- help synthesize new tissues and other amino acids

Protein Structures

A protein is formed from a long polypeptide, which itself consists of amino acids held together in peptide bonds. Over a hundred different amino acids have been identified in nature, twenty of which are part of the human body. All human tissue protein is formed from these twenty primary amino acids through the processes of anabolic synthesis.

Amino acids that can be synthesized within the body in sufficient amounts are considered to be nonessential, or dispensable. The essential aminos must be supplied through dietary sources and are considered to be indispensable. Conditionally essential amino acids are those nonessential aminos that under certain conditions of stress become

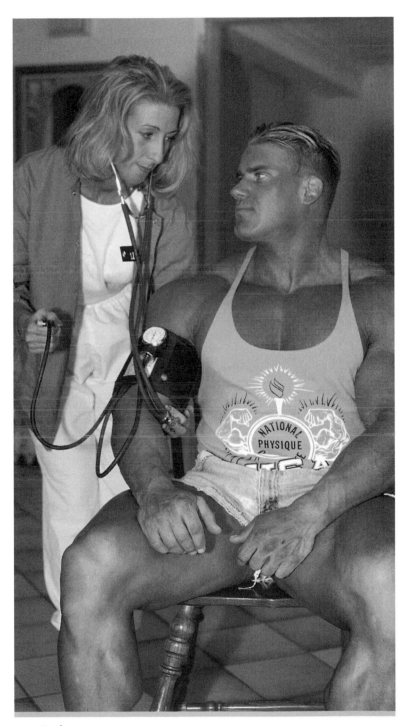

Jay Cutler

Jean-Pierre Fux and Karin Scheuber

essential. They are arginine, glycine, cystine, tyrosine, proline, glutamine, and taurine.

Twenty Primary Amino Acids

1. alanine, Ala	8. glycine, Gly	15. proline, Pro
2. arginine, Arg	9. histidine, His	16. serine, Ser
3. asparagine, Asn	10. isoleucine, Ile	17. threonine, Thr
4. aspartic acid, Asp	11. leucine, Leu	18. tryptophan, Trp
5. cysteine, Cys	12. lysine, Lys	19. tyrosine, Tyr
6. glutamic acid, Glu	13. methionine, Met	20. valine, Val
7. glutamine, Gln	14. phenylalanine, Phe	

Protein Metabolism

After protein has entered the stomach, the major work of breaking whole proteins into smaller peptides and, eventually, free amino acids begins on a large scale. Upon leaving your stomach, many of the amino acids ingested may never reach general circulation because they are needed by organs involved in the metabolic transport process. Amino acids are transported into cells, where tissue synthesis happens and peptide structures are formed, which in turn create more proteins.

The ongoing process of cell repair and synthesis leaves few amino acids for storage inside cells. From a bodybuilder's point of view, there are considerable benefits to ingesting a steady supply of amino acids throughout the day. A good way to do this is to eat six meals a day instead of three. In determining your protein consumption, it is helpful to separate your daily protein needs into two categories: maintenance and growth.

Pirjo Ilkka

Adam Johnson

Estimated Daily Protein Intake by Body Weight
USRDA for protein is 0.8 grams protein/kilo/day

100 lbs/45 kilos

1.5 g protein/k/day = 68 g protein

2.5 g protein/k/day = 113 g protein

3.5 g protein/k/day = 158 g protein

200 lbs/91 kilos

1.5 g protein/k/day = 137 g protein

2.5 g protein/k/day = 228 g protein

3.5 g protein/k/day = 319 g protein

125 lbs/57 kilos

1.5 g protein/k/day = 86 g protein

2.5 g protein/k/day = 143 g protein

3.5 g protein/k/day = 200 g protein

225 lbs/102 kilos

1.5 g protein/k/day = 153 g protein

2.5 g protein/k/day = 255 g protein

3.5 g protein/k/day = 357 g protein

150 lbs/68 kilos

1.5 g protein/k/day = 102 g protein

2.5 g protein/k/day = 170 g protein

3.5 g protein/k/day = 238 g protein

250 lbs/114 kilos

1.5 g protein/k/day = 171 g protein

2.5 g protein/k/day = 285 g protein

3.5 g protein/k/day = 399 g protein

175 lbs/80 kilos

1.5 g protein/k/day = 120 g protein

2.5 g protein/k/day = 200 g protein

3.5 g protein/k/day = 280 g protein

275 lbs/125 kilos

1.5 g protein/k/day = 188 g protein

2.5 g protein/k/day = 313 g protein

3.5 g protein/k/day = 438 g protein

VITAMINS AND MINERALS

Vitamins are organic compounds essential in small amounts for physiologic and metabolic functioning. In terms of dietary volume, vitamins are small; but in terms of value and requirements, vitamins are enormously important. Most vitamins cannot be synthesized by the body and must be obtained from the diet and supplements. The best sources for meeting your vitamin requirements are fresh whole foods. Consistent intake of fresh foods in quantities sufficient for a growing bodybuilder is difficult even in an ideal setting.

Minerals, from the Latin *minera*, meaning *mine*, are inorganic structures required for proper metabolic functioning. Minerals are part of all body tissues and fluids. They are

Art Dykes

important factors in maintaining physiologic processes acting as catalysts in nerve response, muscle contraction, and nutrient metabolism. Minerals are also responsible for the regulation of electrolyte balance. A chronic state of inadequate mineral intake leads to a mineral deficiency. The various symptoms resulting from a mineral deficiency depend on the functions of the element in maintenance and growth.

A mineral is usually referred to by the name of a metal, nonmetal, radical, or phosphate rather than by the name of the compound of which it is a part. Minerals are usually ingested as a compound, such as sodium chloride (table salt), rather than as a free element.

SUPPLEMENTS

Multinutrient Combinations

A multivitamin/mineral combination provides insurance against many areas of dietary deficiency. The range of nutrients included in these broad spectrum multinutrient products is incredible. Some of these supplements are sold in single tablet or capsule form, while others are marketed as multitablet packs. The choice is up to you and is a matter of convenience.

Protein Supplements

Protein supplements are the second most widely used supplement after multivitamins. The largest single financial investment in your bodybuilding career will be protein supplements. Protein supplements are made from several different types of protein sources. In order of decreasing bioavailability these are whey protein, caseinates, eggs, and soy.

Whey Protein

Until about twenty-five years ago, whey was considered a waste product of the dairy industry. Cheese or casein was made from milk, and the by-product of the manufacturing process was whey. The question facing dairy companies was what to do with all that whey.

In its raw state, whey is about 6 percent solids. It is an unappetizing greenish color, looks and tastes terrible, and spoils easily due to its high content of lactose (milk sugar), which is a favorite food of bacteria. Thus, whey didn't appear to hold much commercial promise for dairy

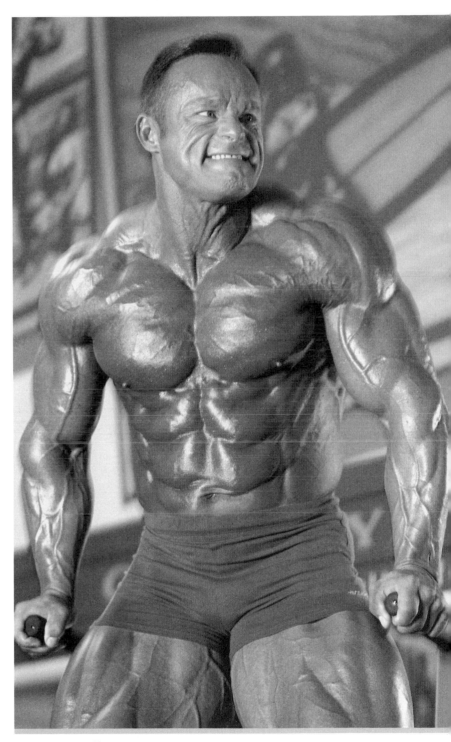

Porter Cottrell

Porter Cottrell

factories, and they simply dumped it in nearby rivers and streams, which quickly led to an environmental hazard due to the high biological oxidation demand of whey solids, something the government frowned on.

Dairy factories began processing whey into a powder containing 11 percent protein, 72 percent lactose, and some ash, or minerals. It was yellow, and it didn't taste great. Some factories persisted in dumping whey, however, including one in Australia that built a pipeline to dump it directly into the ocean.

Eventually, a membrane system was developed to filter whey. The first process, developed by the French, was called ultrafiltration. It involved separating the whey protein from the ash and lactose, which resulted in a protein content of 35 to 70 percent. The process continued to be refined, particularly for the Japanese market, where there is a high tax on the import of any protein food that has a protein content of less than 80 percent. The Japanese were huge consumers of whey because they used it as a substitute for egg whites in certain foods.

Aaron Maddron

B. J. Quinn

The next big break-through in whey processing occurred about fifteen years ago, when a Welsh engineer developed the ion-exchange process. This process revolved around the positive and negative charges, or ion properties, of whey proteins. It featured the use of a resin to isolate the protein material from the whey, adjusting the pH, or acidity level, along the way. This was followed by ultrafiltration methods to further concentrate the protein. He called his product Bipro whey protein isolate. It provided an unprecedented 90 percent protein content while containing less than 1 percent lactose.

The inventor of this ion-exchange process patented its use in all types of applications. Upon later learning that he had terminal cancer, however, the Welshman put his whey patents up for sale. They were purchased by a company that owned a dairy business in Minnesota. That company evolved into Davisco, which today manufactures Bipro. The important point is that this product is a true whey protein isolate, which means that it contains more than 90 percent protein.

B. J. Quinn

Since Davisco now had a lock on the resin method of manufacturing a whey protein isolate, competing dairy companies
sought another way to produce higher-protein whey powders
that wouldn't infringe on patents held by Davisco. Enter
microfiltration, which featured filtering membranes with micro-
scopic holes. Still another process that used even smaller holes
in the filtering membranes for whey was called nanofiltration.
The smaller the holes in the filtering membranes, the more
expensive the process.

The usual whey processing used today involves an initial
ultrafiltration, which brings the protein content to 75 to 80 percent. The resulting whey liquid is run through either micro- or

Jennifer Stimac

Jennifer Stimac

Don Long

nanofiltration, screening out more fat and lactose. That resulting whey has about 1 percent fat and 81 to 86.5 percent protein.

True ion-exchange whey is clear in solution, an advantage if you're using it in bottled protein drinks. This is the Bipro whey, since Bipro's maker, Davisco, still retains the patents for producing ion-exchange whey. Two disadvantages of ion-exchange whey are the high price and limited supply. In addition, studies show that ion-exchange whey protein isolates sometimes contain as much as 70 percent beta-lactoglobulin and as little as 10 percent alpha-lactalbumin. Those percentages aren't even similar to the ones that are naturally found in cow's milk and are significantly different from the proportions found in mother's milk, where alpha-lactalbumin content is high and

Don Long

there is no beta-lactoglobulin present. The significance is that beta-lactoglobulin is considerably more allergenic than alpha-lactalbumin.

The biologically active whey protein fractions, such as lacto-ferrin, are just about nonexistent in true ion-exchange whey protein isolate. This has to do with the processing system used to produce ion-exchange whey, which doesn't favor the retention of the smaller vital whey protein fractions. It's a notable disadvantage because the limited whey fractions have important health benefits.

The primary disadvantage of the filtered whey proteins as opposed to the ion-exchange variety is that the filtered types aren't as pure. True ion-exchange protein—specifically, Bipro—is

Bill Davey

90 percent protein, while filtered whey protein isolates average 86.5 percent protein. The filtered whey also contains slightly higher fat and lactose contents, although the differences aren't significant enough to matter to a consumer.

The advantages of filtered whey proteins include higher levels of valuable whey protein fractions, such as proteose peptone and lactoferrin, and the much heralded glycomacropeptides.

Lactalbumin is often used as a synonym for *whey protein*, which isn't quite correct. In the protein industry the word *lactalbumin* refers to a protein powder manufactured from whey using a high-heat process. Lactalbumin contains abnormally high amounts of heat-denatured beta-lactoglobulin. Since high heat and acid are used in the manufacture of lactalbumin, most of the

Bill Davey

Eric Kaufman

vital whey protein fractions present in the powder become denatured, or broken apart.

The fat bound in the whey protein structure is higher in saturated fat and cholesterol than normal milk fat. The reason you don't often see the true fat content of whey supplements listed is that the bound fat in the whey can only be analyzed by acid hydrolysis, which would denature the native proteins in the whey. The fat content of whey is usually analyzed by ether extraction, which only measures free fat, not the fat bound to proteins. Using the ether extraction technique results in a much lower—though inaccurate—listing of the fat content of a whey protein supplement.

Casein

Contrary to what some people have written, casein isn't a bad protein. It is very stable and resistant to pH or heat denaturation when compared to whey proteins. Many people confuse casein with caseinate, which is made by adjusting the pH of acid casein toward a more neutral level by using an alkali. The resultant caseinate is more soluble in water than acid casein and provides a better texture in food products. Casein, in its native micelle structure, however, forms a stable suspension in water and contains a number of biologically active peptide sequences that could be of great value to athletes. Native micellar casein has a different structure from caseinate and is probably used differently by the body.

Caseinate isn't cheap; it costs more than a whey protein concentrate. From a nutritional standpoint, caseinate has no drawbacks, contrary to what you may read in whey protein ads. Caseinate is considered to be a high-quality protein source. It's just nonsense to suggest that it will cause gas or indigestion any more than whey or other proteins will. In fact, whey proteins are generally thought to be more allergenic in humans than caseinates.

The study quoted in many current whey protein ads compared the metabolic effects of consuming native structure whey proteins and native structure casein in active, fed subjects. It differs from older studies, which often

Eric Kaufman

used fasted subjects, who don't realistically reflect common protein uptake in an athlete's body. The study found that whey protein consumption leads to a rapid but transient increase in plasma amino acid levels and a subsequent stimulation of protein

Darem Charles

synthesis. It also found, however, that amino acid oxidation was increased and that whey protein had no effect at all on catabolic protein breakdown.

The study tells us that when you consume whey protein, it's so rapidly absorbed that much of it is shunted to the liver, where the amino acids are oxidized for energy purposes instead of for synthesizing muscle tissue. The rapid uptake of whey does favor increased protein synthesis. The question, however, is how much of the whey protein is used to make muscle tissue and how much is shunted to the liver for oxidation.

An important and misrepresented conclusion of this study is the author's own statement that whey provides zero anticatabolic effects in the body. Many people have erroneously interpreted that finding to state that consuming larger amounts of whey protein more frequently throughout the day will pro-

Mia Finnegan

vide the same anticatabolic effect as casein did in the study. That isn't what the study showed, though. The author specifically stated that whey protein effected no change in protein breakdown in the body.

In contrast, the same study found that casein consumption led to a lower, slower, and more prolonged appearance of plasma amino acid levels. The authors even stated that the slower amino acid appearance from casein led to a different metabolic response in the body than that of whey protein. Casein consumption slightly increased protein synthesis, and liver oxidation of casein was moderate compared to whey protein.

The important point is that the author clearly said that casein significantly inhibits catabolic protein breakdown in the body. Even more important, the author concluded that casein consumption results in a better net protein balance in the body than you get with whey protein. The study confirmed that whey protein is rapidly absorbed and strongly promotes protein synthesis. At the same time it also found that casein provides a time-released effect and can significantly blunt catabolic protein breakdown.

Human Mother's Milk

Mother's milk contains a balance of 50 to 60 percent whey protein and 40 to 50 percent casein protein. That's a far different balance from what you find in cow's milk, which is about 80 percent

Lovena Stamatiou-Tuley

Jennifer Stimac

casein and 20 percent whey protein. Also, the types of proteins present in the two milks are significantly different. Human mother's milk contains as much as 17 percent lactoferrin, while cow's milk contains about 1 percent lactoferrin. The dominant whey protein fraction in human mother's milk is alpha-lactalbumin, while the dominant whey protein fraction in cow's milk is beta-lactoglobulin.

Human mother's milk doesn't contain any beta-lactoglobulin, a highly allergenic protein in humans compared to alpha-lactalbumin. Nature doesn't do anything by chance, and the high content of lactoferrin found in mother's milk is there for a reason. Among other properties, lactoferrin has antiviral activity and is a potent immune system booster. That's clearly advantageous for newborn humans, who lack full immune system function. From an athletic standpoint, lactoferrin may reduce tissue regrowth

Aaron Maddron

Aaron Maddron

time. Some studies have shown that it may assist in increasing tissue regrowth.

Lactoferrin is one reason that you can't duplicate mother's milk. The cost of purified lactoferrin is prohibitively expensive. Another factor making it difficult to duplicate mother's milk is the beta-lactoglobulin content of cow's whey protein. Infant formula companies have experienced considerable difficulty in making efficacious products from cow's milk protein. In order to make the formula less allergenic to human infants, they usually hydrolyze the whey protein to a high degree. If the beta-lactoglobulin is sufficiently hydrolyzed, its allergenicity in humans is decreased.

It may be difficult to exactly duplicate human mother's milk, but one can at least try to achieve the proper whey-to-casein

Ronnie Coleman

ratio. It's only logical to conclude that if nature makes mother's milk half whey protein and half casein, that ratio is probably best for growing humans.

As we've discussed, whey protein and casein each provides beneficial effects. They're absorbed at different rates and elicit different metabolic responses. They complement each other and should be consumed together for maximum benefit. Recall that mother's milk is roughly 50 percent whey protein and 50 percent casein. Any companies that try to convince you that consuming only whey protein or only casein is the best approach are just blowing smoke. Contrary to what the ads say, there is no scientific basis for their claims. Sure, they can quote many studies, but a closer examination reveals that the studies have little or no applicability in the real world.

Most labels misstate the powder contents, particularly the protein fractions discussed above; take, for instance, glycomacropeptide, which is a hydrolyzed piece of kappa casein. Manufacturers add hydrolyzed whey proteins to their supplements.

The hydrolyzed whey protein may contain pieces of whey peptides that are in the same molecular size range as glycomacropeptides and may even show up on analysis as them, yet they aren't glyco-macropeptides. Despite that fact, the protein supplement labels state that they contain a certain amount of glyco-macropeptides. Such labels are probably misleading because it would be very hard to guarantee a specific glyco-macropeptide content from any current protein source. Also, remember that a true ion-exchange whey protein isolate contains no glyco-macropeptides.

Ronnie Coleman

Complete milk protein is a whole milk protein that is separated from the other constituents of cow's milk by a filtration process. Since no pH changes or excessive heat are used in the processing, the protein retains more of the biologically active protein fractions that are limiting in other protein sources. The casein and whey are in their native, undenatured structures. This is simply protein the way nature intended.

The best protein combination probably involves a filtered milk protein with whey protein concentrate, since you get all the bioactive protein fractions plus both rapid and extended protein activity in the body. The scenario favors increased protein synthesis and a significant anti-catabolic effect.

Will Duggin

Selecting Your Protein Supplement

Contrary to those ubiquitous ads, the type of whey processing, whether filtration or ion-exchange, has little to do with the ultimate quality of the supplement. All changes in pH levels or exposure to high temperatures affect protein quality by promoting denaturation, the permanent breakdown of natural protein structures. It is important to maintain the native structure of the various protein fractions contained in whey as much as possible. Denaturing should be avoided because it minimizes the biological activity of proteins and, therefore, lowers their nutritional value.

The manufacturers who supply the raw protein material vary in their processing techniques, so in many factories each batch of protein may differ in quality from the next. Even the way the cows are fed has an effect on protein quality. All things being equal, the factory supplying the whey determines the quality of the finished product. Some factories use harsher processing techniques that destroy the delicate whey protein fractions. You cannot, however, completely avoid denaturation because of the necessity of killing existing bacteria before filtering the whey. That involves pasteurization, or the use of heat, which unavoidably alters some protein.

As a consumer, you want to look for a company that actively does everything it can to preserve the vital whey protein fractions. Some companies don't bother to analyze the batches of whey they receive and often get their whey from various sources. You also want to look for whey that contains the greatest amounts of those important whey protein fractions. Generally, whey protein concentrate contains more lactoferrin than whey protein isolates. In fact, the concentrates contain double the amount of health-promoting immunoglobulins that isolates have. In addition, the concentrates are less expensive. Thus, from both growth-promoting and health standpoints, whey protein concentrates may be best for bodybuilding purposes.

Whey protein concentrate contains 6 to 7 percent lactose, while whey isolates contain only 1 percent lactose. It sounds significant until you consider that for every 100 grams of whey protein isolate there are 86.5 grams of protein and 1 gram of lactose. For the same quantity of whey protein concentrate, there are 80 grams of

Bill Davey

Dennis James

protein and 6 to 7 grams of lactose. That amount of lactose would probably not approach the threshold that results in symptoms of lactose intolerance.

Biological value (BV) on labels is an attempt to measure how efficiently protein is used in the body. To determine a food's BV, scientists provide a measured intake of protein, then note the nitrogen uptake vs. nitrogen excretion. That's a gross simplification; the actual process is more complex.

In theory, a biological value of 100 is maximal. The BV for whey is often listed at 104, because the extra 4 percent represents a margin of error in the calculation. Even so, biological value is not a universally accepted measure of protein quality because of several factors. For example, BV testing is always done in the fasting state, which affects nitrogen uptake differently from what

Dennis James

takes place when subjects are in a fed state. Simply put, not eating changes the way the body absorbs nitrogen in protein.

The 159 BV for whey you see in some advertisements comes from a study in which the author quoted two earlier researchers who had claimed a 159 BV for whey protein. The problem is, the researchers had confused BV with chemical score, which involves measuring the activity of amino acids in the body. The 159 figure refers to whey's chemical score, not its biological value. A true biological value of 159 for a protein just isn't possible, since the maximum BV is around the 100 mark.

Glutamine
What people should be concerned about is maintaining the health of their intestinal membranes, since that's the area most likely

Mia Finnegan

Mia Finnegan

Porter Cottrell

affected by dietary changes. One way to do that is to take glutamine. The amino acid fuels the regeneration of the intestinal lin-
ing, which breaks down every three days. The body also uses up
available glutamine under high-stress conditions, as it's a favored
fuel of immune cells. Anyone who's under stress, including the
stress of exercise, should aim to take in about 20 to 25 grams
of glutamine daily, divided into smaller doses of about 4 to 5
grams each.

While glutamine makes up half the body's amino acid pool,
whey protein contains about 6 percent peptide-bonded glutamine.
So 100 grams of whey protein provide about 6 grams of glutamine. On the other hand, casein, the other milk protein, naturally
contains 8 to 10 percent glutamine.

The term peptide-bonded glutamine refers to glutamine that is linked to at least one other amino acid via a peptide bond, or peptide chain. The bonded glutamine is superior to L-glutamine, or free glutamine, because the free form of the amino acid is very unstable in the presence of water, heat, and pH changes. The half-life of glutamine in water is comparatively short, which is something to think about the next time you see a drink or protein bar that touts its L-glutamine content.

Peptide-bonded glutamine is far more stable than the free-form variety, able to resist such hostile environments as acid and heat. By the way, peptide-bonded amino acids are always better than free-form amino acids, since free-form amino acids compete with each other for absorption into the body. In contrast, peptide-linked aminos are absorbed by a more orderly and efficient mechanism. Some studies have shown that peptide-bonded glutamine is absorbed as much as ten times more efficiently than L-glutamine into the body.

When you hydrolyze whey protein, you permanently modify the native protein structure, meaning that the protein is denatured

Dan Freeman

Mia Finnegan

and so has little or no biological activity. The hydrolysis process breaks apart peptide bonds, which destroys the protein structure. Even so, you still get the amino acids of whey proteins from the hydrolyzed whey protein. Half the reason to eat proteins is to get those healthful smaller protein chains.

The glycomacropeptide fraction of whey protein stimulates the release of cholecystokinin (CCK) in the gut. CCK may blunt food consumption while also triggering pancreatic digestive enzyme release and insulin secretion. An important—and often overlooked—point, however, is that glycomacropeptides are found only in cheese whey. What's more, it's problematic to say that whey protein helps to suppress appetite. In fact, the human stomach can make glycomacropeptides from casein when casein is consumed in its native structure.

Creatine Monohydrate

Creatine monohydrate is a supplement that many bodybuilders will want to consider taking. This product is meant to be consumed on a daily basis in amounts ranging from 1g to 20 g mixed in water or juice. There is some evidence that creatine monohydrate improves the regeneration of adenosine triphosphate (ATP) within the muscles during intense exercise. The aspect of creatine monohydrate that is most relevant to bodybuilding is the reported increase in muscular size that it imparts to its user. Though creatine monohydrate is not a steroid, its ability to increase muscle size is similar to the effects of some steroids. In most cases, creatine monohydrate is safe to use, as suggested by the manufacturer. The increase in muscle size is due to changes in cellular volume. The body "loads" the creatine into the muscle along with a significant amount of water. This expanded muscle volume appears as increased muscular size and weight.

Bob Weatherill

There is a further potential benefit from using creatine involving the resulting changes in leverage within and between muscle groups due to the increased muscle volume. With better muscle leverage, the amount of resistance used in an exercise can be increased, resulting in new muscle growth.

Hormonal Supplements

There are numerous varieties of hormonal analogues, precursors, agonists, pro-hormones, and so on, that attempt to elevate the body's natural anabolic, or muscle-producing, response. Some of these supplements are effective and others are disappointing. Most of these substances are banned for use in the majority of sports. Many have been sold over the counter as "nutritional supplements." It is still too early to know how they affect long-term health.

DAILY FOOD RECORD

In the attempt to add lean muscle to your body, it eventually becomes a challenge to eat sufficient protein and calories to maintain your existing weight. This is the point at which details count. Keeping a daily food record is crucial to sustained growth, since it enables you to accurately track how well you are keeping up with your dietary plan. The information gathered in your eating record provides the actual daily nutrient numbers, which will be critical for achieving your bodybuilding goals, especially in competition!

CALORIES

To grow, you must stress the muscles through training and eat sufficient food to provide the materials for recovery. The question of how much food to eat in order to gain lean muscle is universal among bodybuilders. Certainly the answer is more food. But how much more? The first step in determining the answer is to calculate how much you are eating now.

As we have just emphasized, the discipline of keeping a daily food record is invaluable. For the purposes of quantifying your current food intake, a fourteen-day span of jotting down everything eaten will suffice. From the time you wake up until going to sleep, keep a record of

1. the time of each meal or snack;
2. what food is eaten; and
3. how much food is eaten (in ounces, pounds, cups, etc.).

At the end of the fourteen-day period, sit down with a pen, piece of paper, calculator, and food value tables (see the end of this chapter for more about food value tables). Estimate the amount of nutrients and calories for each day, and then average the figures over fourteen days. This final calculation will reveal how many grams of protein, carbohydrate, and fat, along with total calories, are supporting your current body weight.

Using the body weight of 200 pounds as an example,

Aaron Maddron

Aaron Maddron

we'll assume that your 200 pounds are supported by the following average daily intake:

3,400 calories—17 calories per pound of body weight

125 g protein—15 percent of daily calories

444 g carbohydrate—52 percent of daily calories

125 g fat—33 percent of daily calories

The ratio of nutrients in this diet is 15 percent protein, 52 percent carbohydrate, 33 percent fat.

What to Eat and How Much

The numbers that the fourteen-day nutrient assessment example reveal are actually healthier than the average person's diet. However, for effective bodybuilding, this diet includes excessive amounts of carbohydrate and fat and insufficient protein. A more effective ratio for muscle growth would be 30 percent protein, 50 percent carbohydrate, 20 percent fat.

At a body weight of 200 pounds, an effective daily intake for bodybuilding is the following:

- 3,400 calories—17 calories per pound of body weight
- 255 g protein—30 percent of daily calories
- 425 g carbohydrate—50 percent of daily calories
- 75 g fat—33 percent of daily calories

The question still remains: How much more do I need to eat above my daily maintenance requirements? The majority of bodybuilders respond efficiently to a 10 percent elevation above their baseline. If this increase proves to be inadequate, then add another 5 percent until you begin to grow to your satisfaction.

Adding 10 percent to the established eating maintenance ratios for 3,400 calories is as follows:

Aaron Maddron

- 3,740 calories—19 calories per pound of body weight
- 280 g protein—30 percent of daily calories
- 468 g carbohydrates—50 percent of daily calories
- 83 g fat—20 percent of daily calories

Aaron Maddron

We advise bodybuilders who have battled against extra body fat to limit their caloric increase to 5 percent or less. Never forget that a pound of body fat contains 3,500 calories. Increasing your food intake too much can quickly add unacceptable amounts of body fat. For example, bumping your daily calories by 20 percent instead of the suggested 10 percent would yield an eleven-day surplus of 3,740 calories. If these extra calories are not burned as energy, then there is only one place for them to go. That's right, the extra calories will be laid down on top of your hard-won muscles. This is not the manner in which you want to build body mass. So, it pays to be cautious when setting up your plan for growth.

TIP FOR PRODUCING MAXIMUM RESULTS FROM YOUR DIET

An established technique for obtaining the optimal response from your newly established growth diet is to eat five to six meals throughout the day, as opposed to merely breakfast, lunch, and dinner. It is important to increase the amount of food you eat during the midmorning, midafternoon, and posttraining times. Of greatest importance is the posttraining meal. During this time, your body is primed from the stress of the workout to literally soak up as would a sponge the proteins and carbohydrates that arrive into circulation.

In the process of becoming an accomplished bodybuilder, one of the pleasant side benefits is gaining intimate knowledge of the nutrient composition of the foods you eat every day of your life. The nutrient composition of foods can be found in food value resource books or tables. One of the best, which we highly recommend, is a modestly priced reference book titled *Food Values of Portions Commonly Used*, by J. E. Pennington (Harper Collins, New York, 1989). The book presents an incredible range of foods and their nutrient composition in an easy-to-use format.

Armin Scholz

Ken Brown

TRAINING

When you think of bodybuilding, you naturally think of going to your local Gold's Gym for a grueling workout. There is great satisfaction received from a well-performed training session. Your muscles are pumped full, and the endorphins are flowing. You're on top of the world. It's time to grow.

Training for growth involves the progressive and consistent increase in your repetitions in an exercise and/or the weight you are using for training. Every possible effort should be made to increase the repetitions to more than twelve, at which point the weight should be periodically increased by approximately 5 percent.

Together in a fine balance, training and recuperation produce the goal of every bodybuilder—expansion of muscle growth. Training is not an inherently complicated process. There are certainly some mistakes that are commonly made, but consistent patience on your part will help you avoid most of these.

The importance of patience in building size cannot be overstated. Size and strength increases can only be coaxed from nature, never forced. It takes very little time to lay down 5 pounds of extra body fat but far longer to gain this much in the form of lean muscle tissue. The general rule in bodybuilding is the harder you train the bigger you'll get. For the most part, this holds true,

Skip La Cour

as long as you attend to the following:

1. eating a sensible diet
2. recovering from one workout to the next
3. increasing the intensity of your training as your body grows

As your bodybuilding experience expands, your body-mind connection will also mature. This mind-muscle gridwork is a vital factor in the essential ability to exert control over a specific muscle group during an exercise.

Growth is the result of an optimal diet and a well-structured training method. The differences between specifically training for size and training for more definition are not great. When your goal is increased muscle mass, you'll focus more of your training attention on foundation exercises such as the squat, bench press, and barbell row. These "major" exercises are also called multi-joint, or compound, movements. The largest muscle groups of the body perform most of the work in this type of movement. In comparison, training for increased definition still includes a major contribution from compound movements but also incorporates additional specific muscle exercises such as concentration curls and rear dumbbell laterals. In addition to a different approach with the weights, training for definition includes an increase in aerobic activity.

In the bodybuilding trade, you must increase the number of repetitions in your exercise or increase the weight being trained with to maintain continued growth. For example, let's say you train legs on Fridays. On a certain Friday, you're able to squat 235 pounds for twelve reps. During the next legs workout, you should increase the weight in your working sets of squats to 245 pounds and attempt to get six good reps. The new weight in the squat of 245 pounds is determined by calculating an increase in the weight that allowed twelve reps by approximately 5 percent.

The workout is motivational fuel for bodybuilders; it's what you think of outside the gym. A bodybuilding workout is seen as pleasure not pain, for it is from the workout that you make your gains. Because you spend a relatively small amount of total weekly time in the gym,

Porter Cottrell

Aaron Maddron

the time spent training must be of maximum efficiency. Important factors to consider when setting up your program are

- how long you've been training (one year vs. five years)
- your degree of success from training (how much muscle you've gained as a gauge of genetic endowment) and recuperative ability
- your goals as a body-builder—size, strength, definition, and competition
- how much work you currently perform in a workout
- how often you work out
- how intense your work-outs are

Initially, the process of setting up an effective train-ing routine can be confusing. For clarity and simplicity, the training routines included in the last chapter of this book are arranged in order of increasing recuperation time between body parts. In other words, the first training routine cycles you through the entire body every four days, providing the least amount of recuperation time between parts of the body. At the opposite end of recuperation time is the group of training programs that train the entire body over twelve days. The twelve-day cycle essentially triples the amount of recuperation time as compared to the briefest cycle of four days. Some individuals will need to exert this type of patience in maintaining a slow, methodical pace of growth.

Most bodybuilders achieve sustainable growth with a training frequency of five to eight days for the completion of all body parts. This pattern allows for adequate recovery time. Total metabolic recovery is more than the disappearance of soreness. Training with sufficient intensity to stimulate growth places huge demands on all of your body's systems. The production of the energy utilized during productive training involves multiple organs and their associated activities. This, in turn, creates a secondary set of recovery objectives for your metabolism to accomplish.

Aaron Maddron

It must be emphasized that in order to grow you must adequately recover from each and every workout. For example, a vicious leg workout on Monday may not appear to affect the muscle groups of the torso; however, if the workload was heavy enough, there is a good chance that your body is going to require a minimum full day of rest between workouts. By increasing or decreasing the frequency of training days and rest days, you can tailor the demands that training places on your body.

MORE IS NOT BETTER

Many times, bodybuilders fall victim to the "more is better" syndrome in their training. The reasoning is that if they gained 5 pounds by training four days per week, averaging twelve sets and eight to twelve reps with each body part, then increasing any or all of these factors will help them grow larger faster.

Bob Weatherill

Perhaps, for a brief period of time, this logic will hold true. However, at some point, more often than not, the progress will grind to a halt. Without your conscious awareness, your body will subtly adjust your intensity level downward to accommodate the energy expenditure involved with longer workouts. As your intensity drops, so will your growth. The end result of more is better training is stagnation.

How do you train harder and still produce consistent gains? This is accomplished by upping the intensity. You can elevate your intensity by reducing time between sets, using more weight without any shift in technique, increasing your effort during the eccentric portion of the movement, and adding one or two assisted repetitions with a training partner. Training intensity can be altered and adjusted within the following areas:

- amount of weight, or resistance
- number of repetitions
- number of sets
- time between sets

Aaron Maddron

- days of training
- sequence of body parts in particular workout

Training intensity can be categorized into three separate areas, listed here in order from least to most stressful:

1. Positive/concentric full repetition momentary failure
2. Positive/concentric full and partial repetition momentary failure
3. Positive/concentric full repetition momentary failure plus additional negative or eccentric-only repetitions

Accordingly, the body's ability to recover (grow) from training decreases as one increases the level of intensity. Thus, the more intensely you train, the more recuperation you require.

Aaron Maddron

Reps (Repetitions) are the single units of motion in a set of an exercise. A repetition is the complete cycle or set of moving the resistance up (concentric) and lowering it back to the starting position (eccentric).

Sets are units of repetitions performed as back-to-back movements. When recording exercises in your notebook, you should indicate the number of sets, reps, and the amount of weight. Most bodybuilders exhibit growth in the range of six to twenty sets per body part for each of the larger muscle groups and three to twelve sets for each of the smaller muscle groups.

Drop Sets are a type of training where at the point of momentary muscular failure (or other prearranged signal), you stop the movement long enough to allow your partner to decrease the weight by a certain amount. The grip and position are maintained while plates are removed or the stack is changed. The extended set is then continued until the point of failure. A slight variation of this approach is down the rack dumbbell sets. In this technique, upon reaching momentary failure in a movement you immediately grab the next lighter set of dumbbells from the rack and use them until once again you reach momentary failure. This descending sequence can be continued until the lightest dumbbells have been used. This technique is often utilized in shoulder or biceps workouts.

Armin Scholz

Rest Pause is similar to drop sets but may be done without the active assistance of partners. At the point of muscular failure, you maintain your grip or position with the resistance load as in drop sets. The weight remains the same without any adjustment from the spotters at hand. Hands remaining in the training position, you "rest" or "pause" for fifteen to thirty-five seconds and then resume the extended set.

Partial Reps involve less-than-full-range repetitions. This shortened range of motion allows you to use heavier-than-normal weights. Partials and half reps are often performed in a weight rack or Smith-type machine.

Half Reps are reps without the top half of the movement, as in curls, or without the bottom half, as in squats.

DURATION OF WORKOUTS

Another aspect of setting up your training program is gauging how long each workout should last. Adjusting training duration is one method of controlling the level of intensity of your workouts. If Day 1 of your training week calls for twenty

Armin Scholz

Ken Brown

total sets in the workout with one partner for seventy minutes, you can increase the intensity of the workout by reducing the total time to sixty minutes for the same number of sets. Intensity is defined as amount of work done in a specific period of time. Performing the same numbers of sets but in less time increases your workload.

In general, it should take about fifty minutes for an individual to train.

On the average for training with one partner, a workout of two to three body parts lasts between sixty and ninety minutes. This is with no additional rest between sets other than the two minutes or so beyond the time to load weights on the bar or machine. It's a tough pace to maintain but not impossible.

The exception to these times are leg workouts. Due to the tremendous amount of energy and oxygen consumed during leg

Aaron Maddron

workouts, in most cases they take the longest time to train correctly. An extreme workout of 100 to 150 minutes is not unheard of. More commonly, a leg workout will take less than ninety-five minutes.

We recommend training with a partner if possible. However, if you do you must allow for a longer workout based on the partner's background and experience. If your workouts regularly take longer than ninety minutes, you should take time to assess how the minutes are actually spent in the gym.

Assisted repetitions and forced repetitions are two brutal training techniques for greatly increasing your level of intensity. However, both are grossly overused by inexperienced bodybuilders. These methods require a partner or two. Moreover, the training partners, or spotters, must have a clear understanding of what you need each of them to do.

Assisted Repetition is a technique in which, as you fail during the positive or concentric portion of the exercise, your partners help assist you to complete the full rep. Correct application of this technique requires experience on the part of your training partners. They must be able to apply just enough help with finishing your rep. If they assist too much, then they are doing the work for you.

Remember that there is no rule that says you must perform bench presses with nothing less than a 45-pound plate on each end. This is too heavy for many novices. If you're new to bodybuilding you must be certain you can do at least eight to ten reps on your own, without any help from the spotters.

Forced Repetition is a technique in which your training partner deliberately applies extra resistance to your reps. The differences between assisted and forced reps are subtle. In assisted reps, your partner applies just enough help to finish the repetition. With forced reps, your partner applies extra resistance by holding back the bar or handles.

Jay Cutler

Slow-Eccentric Repetition is a method for increasing intensity that doubles the time devoted to the eccentric portion of an exercise. Whereas a normal rate of eccentric movement is four seconds for the lowering to be completed, a slow-eccentric movement requires eight seconds.

Michael Ferrante

REPS PER SET

The number of repetitions per set of an exercise is important to focus on when setting up your workouts. There is a wide range of possible rep schemes in bodybuilding. A low rep count is five to six repetitions per set, while a high count is twelve to fifteen reps per set. This is the suggested range of numbers for bodybuilding workouts, not for training for a sport or other specific lifting protocol. A guideline to how many repetitions are appropriate for you is that the heavier the weight, the lower the number of repetitions to expect to perform. The reverse of this is also true—the lighter the weight you are using, the more repetitions you can accomplish.

As important as the reps is your training form. The repetitions must be smooth and controlled. The ideal pace of performing a growth-inducing repetition is two seconds on the lifting (concentric) portion, followed by four seconds for lowering (eccentric) the weight.

In the end, your growth will not depend on having chosen the "perfect" training program but rather on how consistently hard you train using whichever program you pick. One of the biggest mistakes a bodybuilder can make is to switch from one routine to another after only a short while on the first program. There is nothing wrong with changing your training routine, but you should give each one that you start a fair trial period, maybe four to six months.

Alq Gurley

HOW TO SET UP YOUR WORKOUTS

The workout routines laid out in the next chapter are classified according to how many days it takes to accomplish training the full body. Body parts are the categories in which you classify the entire skeletal muscular system into related groups. The body-part categories are chest, back, shoulders (delts), biceps, triceps, thighs, calves, abdominals, and forearms.

A split workout refers to separating the body into different muscle groups. There is less predictable progress when the entire body is trained in a single workout. The simplest split is lower body/upper body. This is followed by push/pull/legs. There are more than 140 different workout splits.

The most productive and practical splits, or categories, are as follows:

    Push (chest, delts, triceps)/pull (back, biceps, traps)/legs
    Chest and triceps/back/shoulders and biceps/legs
    Chest and triceps/back and biceps/shoulders/legs
    Chest/back/shoulders/legs/biceps and triceps
    Chest/back/shoulders/legs/biceps/triceps

These routines take into account the abdominals being trained with each workout, calves trained with legs, and forearms with biceps.

Pirjo Ilokka

A three-day workout cycle is appropriate for the genetic elite. For the remaining 98 percent bodybuilders, the three-day cycle is a recipe for overtraining. The best gains for most bodybuilders are obtained by training with a five- to eight-day cycle. Determining the length of your training cycle is one of the aspects of your bodybuilding avocation that you'll need to adjust through trial and effort. Give each of your workout choices a fair opportunity to produce gains.

The rest of this chapter illustrates how to record the details of an actual workout, in three examples of completed training routines. The examples are in order of increasing duration for a whole-body split to be completed. The same structure can be applied to any of the other workouts that follow in Chapter 6.

EXAMPLE 1

This training cycle involves minimum recuperation time, with the entire body being trained 4 days on and 1 day off.

Mon.	legs: 8 working sets, not including warmup sets
Tues.	push: 12 working sets, not including warmup sets
Wed.	pull: 10 working sets, not including warmup sets
Thurs.	legs
Fri.	off
Sat.	push
Sun.	pull
Mon.	legs
Tues.	push

The following is a detailed description of this training routine's actual exercises with sets and repetitions.

Monday
legs: 8 working sets

All exercises are based upon the maximum weight in the squat that allows for 8 correct repetitions. In this example, 225 pounds will be used for purposes of calculation. This is written as 225/8 (255 pounds for 8 repetitions).

John Sims

Bill Davey and Brandi Hale

When in a working set you're able to perform more than 12 repetitions, add enough weight to allow for a minimum of 6 reps. Warm up by riding a stationary bike for 10 minutes at minimal effort and moderate speed.

Squats: 95/12, 150/10, 175/10, 205/8, 225/maximum reps × 4 sets

Stiff-legged deadlifts: 95/10, 135/8, 175/maximum reps × 2 sets

Leg extensions: 45/12, 90/maximum reps × 2 sets

Leg curls: 75/maximum reps × 1 set

Seated calf raises: 50/12, 80/10, 100/8, 140/maximum reps × 4 sets

Floor crunches: maximum number of reps for each of 5 sets, with 60 seconds of rest between sets

Tuesday
push (chest, shoulders, triceps): 12 working sets

All exercises are based upon the maximum weight in the dip that allows for 8 correct repetitions. In this example, 35 pounds will be used for purposes of calculation. This is written as 35/8.

When in your working sets you're able to perform more than 12 repetitions, add enough weight to allow for a minimum of 6 reps. Warm up by riding a stationary bike for 10 minutes at minimal effort and moderate speed.

Dips: body weight/12, 20/10, 35/maximum reps × 2 sets

Incline dumbbell presses: 25/10, 50/maximum reps × 2 sets

Flat bench dumbbell flyes: 20/10, 40/maximum reps × 1 set

Dumbbell side laterals: 10/12, 25/maximum reps × 2 sets

Rear deltoid dumbbell raises: 10/12, 25/maximum reps × 2 sets

Close-grip bench presses: 75/10, 125/maximum reps × 2 sets

Triceps front cable pressdowns: 80/maximum reps × 2 sets

Machine crunches: 50/maximum reps for 5 sets, with 60 seconds of rest between sets

Art Dykes

Wednesday
pull (back, trapezius, biceps): 10 working sets

All exercises are based upon the maximum weight in the medium-grip front lateral pulldown that allows for 8 correct repetitions. In this example, 150 pounds will be used for purposes of calculation. This is written as 150/8.

When in your working sets you're able to perform more than 12 repetitions, add enough weight to allow for a minimum of 6 reps. Warm up by riding a stationary bike for 10 minutes at minimal effort and moderate speed.

Medium-grip front
  pulldowns: 60/12,
  100/10, 150/maxi-
  mum reps × 2 sets
Seated machine rows:
  100/10, 150/maxi-
  mum reps × 2 sets
Wide-grip front chins:
  body weight/10,
  20/maximum reps ×
  2 sets
Barbell shrugs: 95/12,
  165/10, 225/maxi-
  mum reps × 2 sets

Medium-grip barbell curls: 25/12, 50/10, 95/maximum reps × 4 sets

Leg raises: maximum number of reps for each of 5 sets, with 60 seconds of rest between sets

EXAMPLE 2

This training cycle involves moderately increased recuperation time as compared to Example 1, with the entire body being trained 4 days on and 1 day off but with fewer body parts trained during each workout:

Mon.	legs: 15 working sets
Tues.	chest: 12 working sets
Wed.	back: 15 working sets
Thurs.	shoulders: 10 working sets
Fri.	off
Sat.	biceps: 12 working sets
Sun.	triceps: 12 working sets
Mon.	legs
Tues.	chest

Victor Konovalov

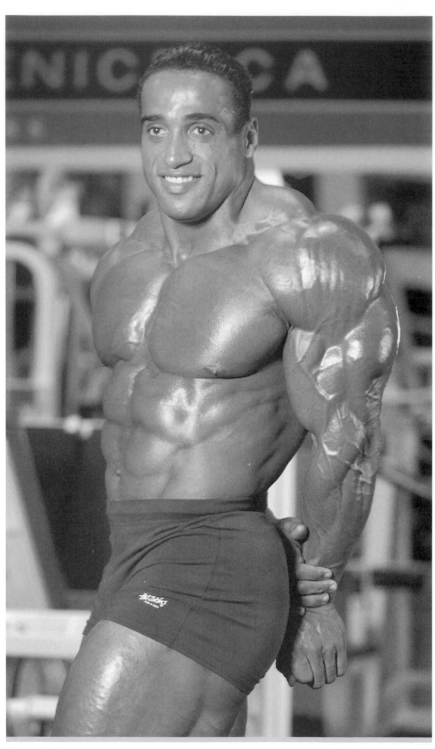

Dennis James

Monday

legs: 15 working sets

All exercises are based upon the maximum weight in the squat that allows for 8 correct repetitions. In this example, 225 pounds will be used for purposes of calculation. This is written as 225/8.

When in your working sets you're able to perform more than 12 repetitions, add enough weight to allow for a minimum of 6 reps. Warm up by riding a stationary bike for 10 minutes at minimal effort and moderate speed.

Squats: 95/12, 150/10, 175/10, 205/8, 225/maximum
  reps × 4 sets
Hack squats: 90/10, 140/maximum reps × 3 sets
Stiff-legged deadlifts: 95/10, 135/8, 175/maximum reps ×
  3 sets
Leg extensions: 45/12, 90/maximum reps × 3 sets
Leg curls: 75/maximum reps × 2 sets
Seated calf raises: 50/12, 80/10, 100/8, 140/maximum
  reps × 4 sets
Floor crunches: maximum number of reps for each of 5 sets,
  with 60 seconds of rest between sets

Tuesday

chest: 12 working sets

All exercises are based upon the maximum weight in the dip that allows for 8 correct repetitions. In this example, 35 pounds will be used for purposes of calculation. This is written as 35/8.

When in your working sets you're able to perform more than 12 repetitions, add enough weight to allow for a minimum of 6 reps. Warm up by riding a stationary bike for 10 minutes at minimal effort and moderate speed.

Dips: body weight/12, 20/10, 35/maximum reps × 4 sets
Incline dumbbell presses: 25/10, 50/maximum reps × 4 sets
Flat bench dumbbell flyes: 20/10, 40/maximum reps × 4 sets
Machine crunches: 50/maximum reps for 5 sets, with 60
  seconds of rest between sets

Dave Hughes

Sylvia Zanet and Andrea Bertona

Ronnie Coleman

Wednesday
back, trapezius: 15 working sets

All exercises are based upon the maximum weight in the medium-grip front lateral pulldown that allows for 8 correct repetitions. In this example, 150 pounds will be used for purposes of calculation. This is written as 150/8.

When in your working sets you're able to perform more than 12 repetitions, add enough weight to allow for a minimum of 6 reps. Warm up by riding a stationary bike for 10 minutes at minimal effort and moderate speed.

Medium grip front pull-downs: 60/12, 100/10, 150/maximum reps × 2 sets

Seated machine rows: 100/10, 150/maximum reps × 2 sets

Wide-grip front chins: body weight/10, 20/maximum reps × 2 sets

Barbell shrugs: 95/12, 165/10, 225/maximum reps × 2 sets

Seated abdominal machine raises: minimum of 20 reps x 5 sets

Thursday

shoulders: 10 working sets

All exercises are based upon the maximum weight in the machine press that allows for 8 correct repetitions. In this example, 150 pounds will be used for purposes of calculation. This is written as 150/8.

When in your working sets you're able to perform more than 12 repetitions, add enough weight to allow for a minimum of 6 reps. Warm up by riding a stationary bike for 10 minutes at minimal effort and moderate speed.

Machine presses: 50/12, 90/10, 130/8, 150/maximum reps × 4 sets

Dumbbell side laterals: 10/12, 25/maximum reps × 3 sets

Rear deltoid dumbbell raises: 10/12, 25/maximum reps × 3 sets

Floor crunches: maximum reps for each of 5 sets, with 60 seconds or less of rest between sets

James Turnage

Agathoklis Agathkleous

Friday
off

Saturday
biceps: 12 working sets

All exercises are based upon the maximum weight in the barbell curl that allows for 8 correct repetitions. In this example, 100 pounds will be used for purposes of calculation. This is written as 100/8.

When in your working sets you're able to perform more than 12 repetitions, add enough weight to allow for a minimum of 6 reps. Warm up by riding a stationary bike for 10 minutes at minimal effort and moderate speed.

> Medium-grip barbell curls: 40/12, 80/10, 100/maximum reps × 5 sets
>
> Incline dumbbell curls: 15/10, 30/maximum reps × 5 sets
>
> Reverse-grip barbell curls: 25/10, 50/maximum reps × 2 sets
>
> Leg raises: maximum number of reps for each of 5 sets, with 60 seconds of rest between sets

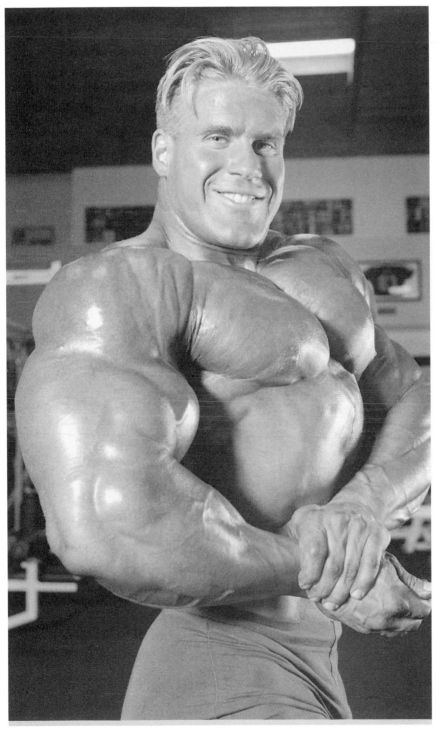

Jay Cutler

Richard Longwidth and Tara Scott

Sunday
triceps: 12 working sets

All exercises are based upon the maximum weight in the reverse-grip bench press that allows for 8 correct repetitions. In this example, 190 pounds will be used for purposes of calculation. This is written as 190/8.

When in your working sets you're able to perform more than 12 repetitions, add enough weight to allow for a minimum of 6 reps. Warm up by riding a stationary bike for 10 minutes at minimal effort and moderate speed.

- Reverse-grip bench presses: 50/12, 100/10, 160/8, 190/maximum reps × 5 sets
- Triceps front cable press-downs: 80/maximum reps × 5 sets
- Close-grip bench presses: 75/10, 125/maximum reps × 2 sets
- Floor crunches: maximum reps for each of 5 sets, with 60 seconds or less of rest between sets

EXAMPLE 3

This training cycle involves significantly increased recuperation time as compared to Examples 1 and 2, with the entire body being trained 3 days on and 2 days off. This allows for an increase in intensity from performing additional work at the end of each working set in the form of a single slow-eccentric repetition.

The unique aspect of this routine is that you do not stop at the point at which you cannot finish the last repetition. There are two steps remaining before the set is completed.

First, when you are unable to move the bar any further, your training partner helps finish the failed rep. He or she is to supply just enough assistance to keep you from struggling with completing the rep. Second, instead of releasing your grip on the bar, your training partner releases his or her grip and you attempt to lower the bar for a count of 8 seconds. In a con-

Christian Boeving

ventional rep, the weight is lowered in 4 seconds. This is called a slow-eccentric repetition. You are to perform only 1 slow-eccentric repetition.

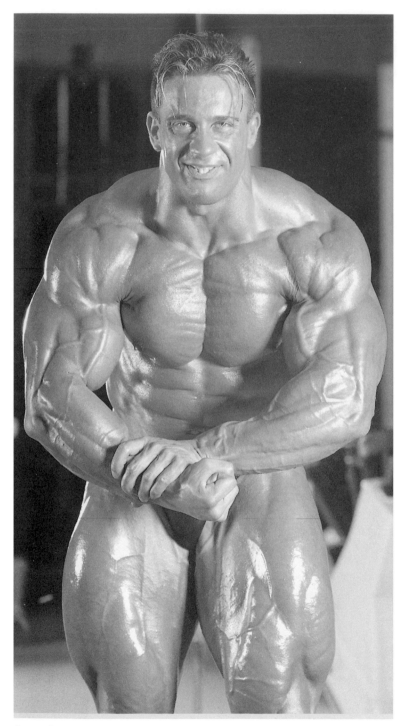

Enzo Ferrari

The magnification of the eccentric aspect of the rep significantly increases the stress on the muscles being trained. When this increase in training stress is followed by sufficient time for metabolic stabilization (recuperation), growth will become manifest.

This training cycle involves 3 days on and 2 days off.

Mon.	legs: 15 working sets
Tues.	chest: 12 working sets
Wed.	back: 15 working sets
Thurs.	off
Fri.	off
Sat.	shoulders: 10 working sets
Sun.	biceps: 12 working sets
Mon.	triceps: 12 working sets
Tues.	off
Wed.	off

Monday
legs: 15 working sets

All exercises are based upon the maximum weight in the squat that allows for 8 correct repetitions. In this example,

John Sims

Todd C. Cummins

225 pounds will be used for purposes of calculation. This is written as 225/8.

When in your working sets you're able to perform more than 12 repetitions, add enough weight to allow for a minimum of 6 reps. Warm up by riding a stationary bike for 10 minutes at minimal effort and moderate speed.

Squats: 95/12, 150/10, 175/10, 205/8, 225/maximum reps × 4 sets + 1 slow-eccentric rep

Hack squats: 90/10, 140/maximum reps × 3 sets + 1 slow-eccentric rep

Stiff-legged deadlifts: 95/10, 135/8, 175/maximum reps × 3 sets

Leg extensions: 45/12, 90/maximum reps × 3 sets + 1 slow-eccentric rep

Leg curls: 75/maximum reps × 2 sets + 1 slow-eccentric rep

Seated calf raises: 50/12, 80/10, 100/8, 140/maximum reps × 4 sets + 1 slow-eccentric rep

Floor crunches: maximum number of reps for each of 5 sets, with 60 seconds of rest between sets

Tuesday

chest: 12 working sets

All exercises are based upon the maximum weight in the dip that allows for 8 correct repetitions. In this example, 35 pounds will be used for purposes of calculation. This is written as 35/8.

When in your working sets you're able to perform more than 12 repetitions, add enough weight to allow for a minimum of 6 reps. Warm up by riding a stationary bike for 10 minutes at minimal effort and moderate speed.

Bill Davey

Dips: body weight/12, 20/10, 35/maximum reps × 4 sets + 1 slow-eccentric rep

Incline dumbbell presses: 25/10, 50/maximum reps × 4 sets + 1 slow-eccentric rep

Flat bench dumbbell flyes: 20/10, 40/maximum reps × 4 sets + 1 slow-eccentric rep

Machine crunches: 50/maximum reps for 5 sets, with 60 seconds of rest between sets

Mia Finnegan

Wednesday
back, trapezius: 15 working sets

All exercises are based upon the maximum weight in the medium-grip front lateral pulldown that allows for 8 correct repetitions. In this example, 150 pounds will be used for purposes of calculation. This is written as 150/8.

When in your working sets you're able to perform more than 12 repetitions, add enough weight to allow for a minimum of 6 reps. Warm up by riding a stationary bike for 10 minutes at minimal effort and moderate speed.

Medium-grip front pulldowns: 60/12, 100/10, 150/maximum reps × 2 sets + 1 slow-eccentric rep

Seated machine rows: 100/10, 150/maximum reps × 2 sets + 1 slow-eccentric rep

Wide-grip front chins: body weight/10, 20/maximum reps × 2 sets + 1 slow-eccentric rep

Barbell shrugs: 95/12, 165/10, 225/maximum reps × 2 sets + 1 slow-eccentric rep

Seated abdominal
machine raises: mini-
mum of 20 reps ×
5 sets

Thursday
off

Friday
off

Saturday
shoulders: 10 working sets

All exercises are based upon
the maximum weight in the
machine press that allows for
8 correct repetitions. In this
example, 150 pounds will be
used for purposes of calculation. This is written as 150/8.

When in your working
sets you're able to perform
more than 12 repetitions, add
enough weight to allow for a
minimum of 6 reps. Warm up
by riding a stationary bike for
10 minutes at minimal effort
and moderate speed.

Shonna McCarver

Machine presses: 50/12,
90/10, 130/8, 150/maximum reps × 4 sets + 1 slow-
eccentric rep
Dumbbell side laterals: 10/12, 25/maximum reps × 3 sets +
1 slow-eccentric rep

Jay Cutler

Rear deltoid dumbbell
raises: 10/12,
25/maximum reps
× 3 sets + 1 slow-
eccentric rep
Floor crunches: maxi-
mum reps for each of
5 sets, with 60 sec-
onds or less of rest
between sets

Sunday
biceps: 12 working sets

All exercises are based upon
the maximum weight in the
barbell curl that allows for 8
correct repetitions. In this
example, 100 pounds will be
used for purposes of calculation. This is written as 100/8.

When in your working
sets you're able to perform
more than 12 repetitions, add
enough weight to allow for a
minimum of 6 reps. Warm up
by riding a stationary bike for
10 minutes at minimal effort
and moderate speed.

Medium-grip barbell
curls: 40/12, 80/10,
100/maximum reps
× 5 sets + 1 slow-
eccentric rep

Michael Ferrante

Michael Ferrante

Incline dumbbell curls: 15/10, 30/maximum reps × 5 sets
+ 1 slow-eccentric rep

Reverse-grip barbell curls: 25/10, 50/maximum reps × 2 sets
+ 1 slow-eccentric rep

Leg raises: maximum number of reps for each of 5 sets, with
60 seconds of rest between sets

Monday
triceps: 12 working sets

All exercises are based upon the maximum weight in the reverse-grip bench press that allows for 8 correct repetitions. In this example, 190 pounds will be used for purposes of calculation. This is written as 190/8.

When in your working sets you're able to perform more than 12 repetitions, add enough weight to allow for a minimum of 6 reps. Warm up by riding a stationary bike for 10 minutes at minimal effort and moderate speed.

Reverse-grip bench presses: 50/12, 100/10, 160/8,
190/maximum reps × 5 sets + 1 slow-eccentric rep

Triceps front cable pressdowns: 80/maximum reps × 5 sets
+ 1 slow-eccentric rep

Close-grip bench presses: 75/10, 125/ maximum reps × 2
sets + 1 slow-eccentric rep

Floor crunches: maximum reps for each of 5 sets, with 60
seconds or less of rest between sets

Tuesday
off

Wednesday
off

Gunther Schlierkamp

THE WORKOUTS

Over 3 days: 4 days on and 1 day off

Mon.	legs
Tues.	push
Wed.	pull
Thurs.	legs
Fri.	off
Sat.	push
Sun.	pull
Mon.	legs
Tues.	push

Over 4 days: 4 days on and 2 days off

Mon.	legs
Tues.	push
Wed.	pull
Thurs.	legs
Fri.	off
Sat.	off
Sun.	push
Mon.	pull
Tues.	legs
Wed.	push

Adam Johnson

Over 4 days: 2 days on and 1 day off

Mon.	legs
Tues.	push
Wed.	off
Thurs.	pull
Fri.	legs
Sat.	off
Sun.	push
Mon.	pull

Over 4 days: 3 days on and 1 day off

Mon.	legs
Tues.	push
Wed.	pull
Thurs.	off
Fri.	legs
Sat.	push
Sun.	pull

Over 5 days: 4 days on and 1 day off

Mon.	legs
Tues.	chest, triceps
Wed.	back
Thurs.	shoulders, biceps
Fri.	off
Sat.	legs
Sun.	chest, triceps
Mon.	back
Tues.	shoulders, biceps

Over 5 days: 2 days on and 2 days off

Mon.	legs
Tues.	push
Wed.	off
Thurs.	off
Fri.	pull
Sat.	legs
Sun.	off
Mon.	off
Tues.	push
Wed.	pull
Thurs.	off
Fri.	off
Sat.	legs

Over 5 days: 3 days on and 1 day off

Mon.	legs
Tues.	chest, triceps
Wed.	back
Thurs.	off
Fri.	shoulders, biceps
Sat.	legs
Sun.	chest, triceps
Mon.	off

Over 6 days: 4 days on and 1 day off

Mon.	legs
Tues.	chest
Wed.	back
Thurs.	shoulders
Fri.	off
Sat.	arms

Aaron Baker

Skip La Cour

Sun.	legs
Mon.	chest
Tues.	back

Over 6 days: 4 days on and 2 days off

Mon.	legs
Tues.	chest, triceps
Wed.	back
Thurs.	shoulders, biceps
Fri.	off
Sat.	off
Sun.	legs
Mon.	chest, triceps
Tues.	back
Wed.	shoulders, biceps

Over 6 days: alternating days over 6 days

Mon.	legs
Tues.	off
Wed.	push
Thurs.	off
Fri.	pull
Sat.	off
Sun.	legs

Over 6 days: 2 days on and 1 day off

Mon.	legs
Tues.	chest, triceps
Wed.	off
Thurs.	back
Fri.	shoulders, biceps

Sat.	off
Sun.	legs
Mon.	chest, triceps

Over 6 days: 3 days on and 1 day off

Mon.	legs
Tues.	chest
Wed.	back
Thurs.	off
Fri.	shoulders
Sat.	arms
Sun.	legs
Mon.	off

Over 6 days: 3 days on and 2 days off

Mon.	legs
Tues.	push
Wed.	pull
Thurs.	off
Fri.	off
Sat.	legs

Over 7 days: 4 days on and 1 day off

Mon.	legs
Tues.	chest
Wed.	back
Thurs.	shoulders
Fri.	off
Sat.	biceps
Sun.	triceps
Mon.	legs
Tues.	chest

Scott Hagan

Jonathan Lawson

Jonathan Lawson

Jay Cutler

Over 7 days: 4 days on and 2 days off

Mon.	legs
Tues.	chest
Wed.	back
Thurs.	shoulders
Fri.	off
Sat.	off
Sun.	arms
Mon.	legs
Tues.	chest
Wed.	back
Thurs.	off
Fri.	off

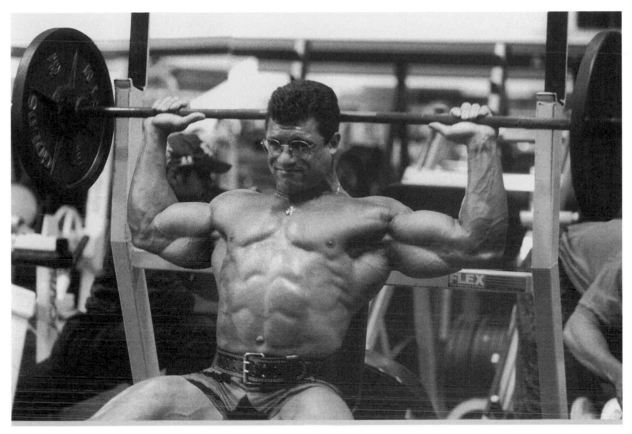

Ronnie Schweyher

Sat.	shoulders
Sun.	arms
Mon.	legs
Tues.	chest

Over 7 days: 3 days on and 4 days off

Mon.	legs
Tues.	push
Wed.	pull
Thurs.	off
Fri.	off
Sat.	off
Sun.	off

Debbie Kruck

Over 7 days: 4 days on and 3 days off

Mon.	legs
Tues.	chest, triceps
Wed.	back
Thurs.	shoulders, biceps
Fri.	off
Sat.	off
Sun.	off

Over 7 days: 5 days on and 2 days off

Mon.	legs
Tues.	chest
Wed.	back
Thurs.	shoulders
Fri.	arms
Sat.	off
Sun.	off

Over 7 days: 2 days on and 1 day off

Mon.	legs
Tues.	chest
Wed.	off
Thurs.	back
Fri.	shoulders
Sat.	off
Sun.	arms
Mon.	legs

Over 6 days: 3 days on and 2 days off

Mon.	legs
Tues.	chest, triceps

Wed.	back
Thurs.	off
Fri.	off
Sat.	shoulders, biceps
Sun.	legs

Over 8 days: 4 days on and 2 days off

Mon.	legs
Tues.	chest
Wed.	back
Thurs.	shoulders
Fri.	off
Sat.	off
Sun.	biceps
Mon.	triceps
Tues.	legs
Wed.	chest
Thurs.	off
Fri.	off
Sat.	back
Sun.	shoulders
Mon.	biceps
Tues.	triceps

Over 8 days: alternating days on and off

Mon.	legs
Tues.	off
Wed.	chest, triceps
Thurs.	off
Fri.	back
Sat.	off
Sun.	shoulders, biceps
Mon.	off
Tues.	legs

Bob Weatherill

Mia Finnegan

Mia Finnegan

Dr. Christine Lydon

Over 8 days: 2 days on and 2 days off

Mon.	legs
Tues.	chest, triceps
Wed.	off
Thurs.	off
Fri.	back
Sat.	shoulders, biceps
Sun.	off
Mon.	off
Tues.	legs

Dr. Christine Lydon

Over 8 days: 3 days on and 1 day off

Mon.	legs
Tues.	chest
Wed.	back
Thurs.	off
Fri.	shoulders
Sat.	biceps
Sun.	triceps
Mon.	off
Tues.	legs

Jonathan Lawson

Over 7 days: 3 days on and 2 days off

Mon.   legs
Tues.   chest
Wed.   back
Thurs. off
Fri.   off
Sat.   shoulders
Sun.   arms
Mon.   legs

Jonathan Lawson

Over 9 days: 2 days on and 2 days off

Mon.	legs
Tues.	chest
Wed.	off
Thurs.	off
Fri.	back
Sat.	shoulders
Sun.	off
Mon.	off
Tues.	arms
Wed.	legs

Dennis James

Over 9 days: 2 days on and 1 day off

Mon.	legs
Tues.	chest
Wed.	off
Thurs.	back
Fri.	shoulders
Sat.	off
Sun.	biceps
Mon.	triceps
Tues.	off
Wed.	legs

Over 9 days: 3 days on and 2 days off

Mon.	legs
Tues.	chest
Wed.	back
Thurs.	off
Fri.	off
Sat.	shoulders
Sun.	biceps
Mon.	triceps
Tues.	off
Wed.	off
Thurs.	legs

Over 10 days: alternating days on and off

Mon.	legs
Tues.	off
Wed.	chest
Thurs.	off
Fri.	back
Sat.	off
Sun.	shoulders
Mon.	off
Tues.	arms
Wed.	off
Thurs.	legs

Dennis James

Art Dykes

Over 12 days: 2 days on and 2 days off

Mon.	legs		Mon.	off
Tues.	chest		Tues.	biceps
Wed.	off		Wed.	triceps
Thurs.	off		Thurs.	off
Fri.	back		Fri.	off
Sat.	shoulders		Sat.	legs
Sun.	off			

Over 12 days: alternating days
on and off

Mon.	legs
Tues.	off
Wed.	chest
Thurs.	off
Fri.	back
Sat.	off
Sun.	shoulders
Mon.	off
Tues.	biceps
Wed.	off
Thurs.	triceps
Fri.	off
Sat.	legs

Art Dykes

INDEX

Split workouts, 111
Supplements. *See also* Protein supplements
   multinutrient combinations, 56

Taurine, 52
Ten-day workout schedules, 157
Three-day workout schedules, 139
Training, 19, 95–109
   assisted repetitions, 106–7
   drop sets, 103
   forced repetitions, 107
   half repetitions, 104
   intensity, 102
   "more is better" syndrome, 100–104
   partial repetitions, 104
   with partners, 106
   patience in, 95
   repetitions (reps), 102–3
   rest pause, 104
   setting up program, 98–100
   slow-eccentric repetitions, 107
   workout duration, 104–7
Trapezius workouts, 122, 132–33
Triceps workouts, 124, 137
Twelve-day workout schedules,
   158–59
Tyrosine, 52

Ultrafiltration of whey protein, 58

Videos for self-assessment, 17
Vitamins in diet, 55–56

Weight, self-assessment of, 14
Whey protein, 57–68, 79
Bipro, 60, 65
   filtered, 65–66
   ion-exchange process, 60, 64
   microfiltration, 61
   ultrafiltration, 58
Whey protein isolate, 60
Workout schedules, 139–59
   three-day, 139
   four-day, 139–40
   five-day, 140–41
   six-day, 141–43
   seven-day, 143, 146–48, 154
   eight-day, 149, 152–53
   nine-day, 155–56
   ten-day, 157
   twelve-day, 158–59
Workouts
   cycle, 112
   duration, 104–7
   setup, 111–37